ATTENTION
DEFICIT
HYPERACTIVITY
DISORDER

Brian Jacobs and Lorna Miles

Published by
British Association for Adoption & Fostering
(BAAF)
Saffron House
6–10 Kirby Street
London EC1N 8TS
www.baaf.org.uk

Charity registration 275689 (England and Wales)
and SC039337 (Scotland)

British Library Cataloguing in Publication Data
A catalogue record for this book is available from the British Library

ISBN 978 1 907585 48 7

Project management by Jo Francis, Publications Department, BAAF
Designed and typeset by Fravashi Aga
Printed in Great Britain by the Lavenham Press

BAAF is the leading UK-wide membership organisation for all those
concerned with adoption, fostering and child care issues.

Contents

Note about the authors

Brian Jacobs is a Consultant Child and Adolescent Psychiatrist who has specialised in working with children who have complex neuropsychiatric disorders in inpatient and outpatient settings in the South London and Maudsley NHS Trust for the past twenty years. Prior to that, he worked at Queen Mary's Hospital for Children in Carshalton. He has particular interests in training future child psychiatrists and actively works to support this across Europe.

Lorna Miles is an adoptive parent and has been a foster carer on and off for 25 years. In addition, she has worked with children in care in a variety of settings. She is involved in training foster carers and since the publication of *Holding on and Hanging in* by BAAF in 2010, she has been running workshops on attachment.
www.lornamiles.co.uk.

The series editor

The editor of this series, **Hedi Argent**, is an established author/editor for BAAF. Her books cover a wide range of family placement topics; she has written several guides and a story book for young children.

Looking behind the label...

Jack has mild learning difficulties and displays some characteristics of ADHD and it is uncertain whether this will increase...

Beth and Mary both have a diagnosis of global developmental delay...

Abigail's birth mother has a history of substance abuse. There is no clear evidence that Abigail was prenatally exposed to drugs but her new family will have to accept some kind of developmental uncertainty...

Jade has some literacy and numeracy difficulties, but has made some improvement with the support of a learning mentor...

Prospective adopters and carers are often faced with the prospect of having to decide whether they can care for a child with a health need or condition they know little about and have no direct experience of. No easy task...

Will Jack's learning difficulties become more severe?
Will Beth and Mary be able to catch up?
When will it be clear whether or not Abigail has been affected by parental substance misuse?
And will Jade need a learning mentor throughout her school life?

It can be difficult to know where to turn for reliable information. What lies behind the diagnoses and "labels" that many looked after children bring with them? And what will it be like to live with them? How will they benefit from family life?

Parenting Matters is a unique series, "inspired" by the terms used – and the need to "decode them" – in profiles of children needing new permanent families. Each title provides expert knowledge about a particular condition, coupled with facts, figures and guidance presented in a straightforward and accessible style. Each book also describes what it is like to parent an affected child, with adopters and foster carers "telling it like it is", sharing their parenting experiences, and offering useful advice. This combination of expert information and first-hand experiences will help readers to gain understanding, and to make informed decisions.

Titles in the series will deal with a wide range of health conditions and steer readers to where they can get more information. They will offer a sound introduction to the topic under consideration and offer a glimpse of what it would be like to live with a "labelled" child. Most importantly, this series will look behind the label and give families the confidence to look more closely at a child whom they otherwise might have passed by.

Keep up with new titles as they are published by signing up to our newsletter on www.baaf.org.uk/bookshop.

Shaila Shah

Introduction

This book is concerned with Attention Deficit Hyperactivity Disorder (ADHD), and the special needs of children, particularly adopted and looked after children, who have this condition.

The first half of the book starts with a short explanation of ADHD and related conditions in children and young people: symptoms, prognosis and treatment are outlined clearly and simply. It goes on to look at the different ways in which ADHD can affect child development and behaviour; the issues it raises with regard to educational provision for affected children; and where and how to get help for children with ADHD.

The second half of the book tells the story of Lorna Miles and her experiences of parenting a child with ADHD, and how this affected day-to-day family life.

UNDERSTANDING ATTENTION DEFICIT HYPERACTIVITY DISORDER (ADHD)

BRIAN JACOBS

CHAPTER 1

What is ADHD?

Introduction

ADHD (Attention Deficit Hyperactivity Disorder) is a diagnosis that leads to strong feelings in parents, teachers, members of the public and the press. These tend to range from blaming the parents – 'If the child is badly behaved, it must obviously be the parents' fault' – through conviction that it must be due to what the child is eating (colourings, sugar and food additives) to the horror at the dreadful doctors suggesting medication – 'They'll turn him into a zombie'; 'They'll take her character away'; 'They'll poison his brain'.

ADHD consists of difficulties for the child in three core symptoms:

- Attention difficulties: the child cannot concentrate and attend to tasks. He may appear not to listen and is often forgetful. He finds tasks that involve sustaining attention for any length of time particularly difficult.

● Impulsivity: the child has difficulty waiting their turn. He will shout out answers without being asked, interrupt when others are speaking and act without thinking.

● Hyperactivity/hyperkinesis: the child has difficulty staying still, will constantly fidget, play with their hands and acts as if "driven by a motor". He will leave his seat in the classroom and tend to run about and climb. The child will have difficulty playing quietly.

In Europe, the formal name of the disorder is **hyperkinetic disorder**. It is defined in the International Classification of Diseases ICD-10 of the World Health Organisation (WHO, 1992). The rules for making the diagnosis require the difficulties to be seen regularly in at least two different environments in the child's life, e.g. at home and at school.

In the United States, a similar pattern of difficulties is known as **ADHD**. The diagnostic rules in the US are different and lead to a classification with sub-types of the disorder; they do not require all of the three components to be present at the same time. Neither do the difficulties have to be seen in more than one context in the child's life. This contributes to a larger group of children receiving the diagnosis. However, the matter is complicated because professionals in the UK have slipped into referring to the condition as "ADHD" without distinguishing to which of the two groups they are referring. This can lead to confusion.

In this chapter, I use the term ADHD except at points when it is important to distinguish between the two groups.

How common is the disorder?

A number of studies suggest that in primary school-aged children, hyperkinetic disorder is seen at a rate of about 1.5 per cent (Taylor, 2007, pp 10–11). There are more boys than girls with the disorder at any one time (ratio about 3:1). Using the US criteria, the level rises to about five per cent. The condition is under-diagnosed in the UK; this is revealed by comparing the rates found in population research studies with the numbers that are seen by GPs and in paediatric and Child and Adolescent Mental Health Services (CAMHS), which are much lower. This rate of diagnosis has improved in recent years but is still an issue (e.g. Sayal et al, 2002). The recognition of the disorder is increasing in the UK, and it is now diagnosed at about a rate of three in a thousand children. However, this is still only about a fifth of the more severe form of the disorder (hyperkinetic disorder) and six per cent of the overall rate diagnosed when the US criteria are used. It means that a lot of children are having the wrong reasons given for their difficult behaviour and may well not be offered appropriate interventions. As Collishaw and colleagues point out (2004), in studies of successive groups of the population at risk over a 25-year period, the rates of hyperactivity have remained rather stable while the rates of some other common disorders such as conduct disorders and emotional disorders have increased (Taylor, 2007, p 12).

ADHD has to be distinguished from the normal exuberance and energy shown by young children. This may be a particular issue for older parents and foster carers whose own energy levels may not be quite what they once were. A useful way for parents or carers to identify that your child *may* have the disorder is to compare your child with a range of other children, not just the one calm child who lives next door or the one other hyperactive child who is a friend. Once children are in primary school, teachers may pick out your child as having difficulties. However, teachers are often reluctant to name the difficulties: they want to maintain a positive outlook; they believe in the child's ability to grow and mature. This can lead to minimising difficulties that are obvious to the teacher when they come to talk to parents and carers.

The disorder is particularly under-diagnosed among girls, preschoolers, adolescents and where symptoms of inattention are more marked than those of hyperactivity (Sayal, 2007).

What are the causes of ADHD?

These are summarised in accessible form in the NICE Guideline for ADHD (NICE, 2008, pp 29–30). There are a variety of biological risk factors, including drug (heroin and cocaine in particular) or alcohol misuse during pregnancy. Smoking and lack of oxygen to the foetus are also risk factors during pregnancy. Some genetic conditions such as Fragile X (a condition involving changes in the X chromosome – the most common factor in inherited intellectual disability) and neurofibromatosis (a congenital condition, typified by benign tumours) are also known risks. Other conditions such as epilepsy or traumatic head injury can also lead to the ADHD pattern.

There has been a widespread belief that food additives are strongly linked to ADHD, but the evidence for this is limited.

McCann and colleagues (2007) completed a double-blinded placebo-controlled crossover trial of food additives in three-year-old and eight/nine-year-old children. This study confirmed the association between food additives (artificial colours, sodium benzoate or both) and increased levels of ADHD symptoms in the child populations studied. Studies indicate short-term toxic effects of food additives on the level of ADHD symptoms in children whether they have ADHD or not, and might contribute towards significant impairment in some cases. There is no indication that food additives cause long-term effects on child development (NICE, 2008, p 114).

Two studies have suggested that maternal anxiety during pregnancy affects the rate of ADHD in the child. One of these studies suggested that it accounts for about a fifth of risk, but the other group suggests a lower figure of five–ten per cent (O'Connor et al, 2002).

There is little evidence that poor parenting causes ADHD – although it can exacerbate it. On the other hand, severe, chronic institutional upbringing (e.g. Romanian orphanages) can lead to ADHD (Rutter et al, 2002).

There is evidence in children diagnosed with ADHD of brain dysfunction in the prefrontal cortex and striatum (planning deficits); the thalamus and cerebellum (timing difficulties); the orbitofrontal cortex (difficulty in postponing immediate rewards for greater gain): i.e. the suggested deficits from psychological research and genetic research are complex in their interactions (Taylor and Sonuga-Barke, 2008, p 531). The suggested mechanisms involve the amine transmitters that carry messages between cells such as noradrenaline and dopamine. It is rather likely that there are several variant pathways involving chemical transmitter imbalance and relative low function in inhibitory pathways. This fits with the genetic finding that there are a number of different transporter and receptor gene effects where each slight variation in DNA sequences leads to modest changes in the level of hyperactivity so that there are likely to be interactive effects. Unfortunately, there is no straightforward account of the research base to these statements in layperson's language. For the adventurous, Curran (2007) provides a relatively accessible account.

SECTION I

CHAPTER 2

Symptoms, prognosis and treatment

There are no symptoms of ADHD that occur only in that specific condition, so this means that to make a diagnosis requires careful assessment by a specialist, a child psychiatrist, a paediatrician or a child and adolescent clinical psychologist. As will be seen below, the matter is further complicated because some of the symptoms are seen in other child mental health disorders. Furthermore, ADHD can occur alongside other child psychiatric diagnoses, a situation referred to as co-morbidity.

When there is a possibility of a child having ADHD, parents and carers want professionals to take the behaviours they describe seriously (ADDISS, 2003). Parents, carers and teachers should not be put off from considering whether a child should be referred by their GP for assessment.

Symptoms of ADHD

The symptom groups, which were listed earlier, are now described in more detail.

Attention difficulties

The aim here is to think about whether your child is having difficulties that interfere with their ability to do certain things that other parents take for granted in their children of a similar age and ability. Does the difficulty which you think your child has interfere with their ability to enjoy an activity, to learn from it or to complete the activity or task? This can sound as though everything that a child is engaged in should be seen as educational, but that is not what I mean here.

Example

Watching television: how long can your child sit and watch TV? You would expect that a younger child might not be able to sit for as long as an older child. This will depend to some extent on the age-appropriateness of the programme. Most children can sit for 15 minutes or longer. If the programme is about something that they are particularly interested in, some children who are hyperactive will achieve this, but not otherwise.

There are important general lessons here. Firstly, that children will vary in how long they will attend to an activity depending on its interest for them; and secondly, that there is no absolute measure that distinguishes the hyperactive child in all circumstances from the child who does not have these problems.

If your child can read on his own, how long can he do this without moving on to another activity? Similar questions can be asked about his ability to play with a particular toy or group of toys by himself and with others. As a rule of thumb (only), a school-aged child will normally be able to settle to an activity for 15 minutes provided it is within their ability. If it is above their ability, most children will drift to other things quickly.

Parents and carers may also think about their child's ability to attend to daily family tasks such as laying the table, tidying, washing up, etc. If your child is reluctant to take part, makes lots of mistakes, complains a lot, is "unwilling" to follow calmly given, simple instructions and does not complete the task, this may suggest that ADHD is a possible explanation (among several explanations), if other relevant behaviours are also present. You will see that similar self-questioning can be used by teachers about your child's behaviour in school during lessons. But the behaviours listed are non-specific and may also point to other problems such as oppositional defiant disorder, or could suggest that a child has learning difficulties.

Another feature of attention deficit is that the child has great difficulty in self-organisation, e.g. taking the correct things to school and remembering to bring them home again. They often lose things at home and at school, and tend to be forgetful. Parents or carers often complain that the child cannot pack their school bag, although she will claim to have done so.

Impulsivity

This can be difficult to distinguish from attention difficulties on the one hand, and from motor hyperactivity on the other. The central question is whether the child tends to act without thinking when other children of the same age and ability would not do so. Some situations can help parents, carers and teachers to recognise this feature:

- Does the child often interrupt others who are speaking?

- Do they blurt out the answers to questions in a setting where they would know that the rules expect them to wait their turn?

- Do they talk excessively, for example, more than half the time when playing with another child or by themselves?

- Do they talk at the dinner table to a similar extent with little regard for others, or make a lot of noise for a large proportion of the time or in inappropriate situations? 'She is unable to contain herself,' you may say. This is a warning signal but no more. There is a fine balance between an exuberant, happy child and one who is unable to "give and take" in conversation.

In each situation, you should ask yourself whether your child does this more than other children or not. All children get excited at times, as do many adults. What you are trying to distinguish is when it is more and different.

Hyperactivity

Hyperactive children fiddle and fidget, with restless hands or feet. Of course, children fidget for other reasons as well, but teachers often complain that the child leaves their seat frequently and wanders about the class. Your child may seem always to be "on the go" – some describe this "as if driven by a motor". They find it difficult to play quietly and may talk excessively (much more than most of their peers). They may be able to sit and watch TV but will often be restless and move around even while remaining seated. The restlessness may even happen when the child is asleep, with excessive tossing and turning.

One activity that doctors have learned to ignore is the child's ability to play computer games. This activity appears to have so

13

much relevance for children in general, that otherwise restless children seem to be able to attend and concentrate whilst often sitting relatively still. Another time when the child may show fewer of their symptoms is in a strange situation, particularly if it is a first-time experience. We have learned to recognise that this may happen when the child pays a first visit to the specialist doctor.

Associated features

As Taylor notes (2007, p 7), although these features may commonly be seen in ADHD, they are not part of the defining symptoms and are also frequently seen in other child mental health disorders. They include:

- sleep disturbance: the child goes to sleep very late or in the early hours and may wake frequently during the night;

- noncompliance: the child will not do what they are told;

- aggression: this can take the form of flaring anger with little provocation (temper tantrums) and may result in verbal aggression (swearing and being offensive) or physical violence;

- clumsiness;

- reading difficulties;

- emotional outbursts.

Treatments for ADHD

Psychological interventions

1) Explanation
Treatment should begin with discussion about the disorder with parents and carers and with the child at an age-appropriate level.

If the child or young person is old enough, this needs to take account of their subjective experiences as well as those of the parents or carers.

2) Parent training

This should be the first line of intervention to help the parents or carers of children with mild to moderate ADHD. For hyperkinetic disorder (ADHD that is impacting on the child's life in two different settings, such as home and school), parent training should form a component of treatment, but in such cases, outcomes are likely to be greatly improved by the added use of medication (as becomes apparent in Lorna Miles' story, in Section II of this book).

There are a variety of evidence-based programmes now to help parents and carers. Most are delivered in a group format – not only because it is more efficient, but also because it allows parents to learn from each other, which is a very powerful and supportive process. They learn from each other in ways that professionals would be hard-pressed to match. These programmes mostly last for around 10–12 sessions of about two hours each. They involve teaching skills, rehearsing them and practising them between sessions as well as problem-solving the difficulties that inevitably arise when a technique does not go according to plan. Examples of such training include *The Incredible Years* (www.incredibleyears.com/) and *1,2, 3 Magic* (www.parentmagic.com/). Each of these programmes also has a version to help teachers with classroom management and provides books that are full of useful advice. Taylor (2007, pp 23–4) gives alternatives to these programmes.

Parents and carers may find that revisiting such training as the child becomes a bit older can also be helpful. The material or the principles behind it can be taught on a one-to-one basis. Doing so may be appropriate in special circumstances.

SECTION I

3) Behaviour therapy

This has an evidence base for working with the parents or carers and with the child, or with the family together, when ADHD is the presenting problem. The principles do not differ from those applied to most other childhood mental health difficulties, but as ADHD makes it harder for the child not to react impulsively to situations, this needs to be taken into account.

Example

A five- to seven-year-old child with ADHD, when playing "aeroplanes", is likely to do the actions of flying their plane fast and then quickly crashing it. When playing with this child, the parent might slow down their own plane's flight and land it safely, rescuing the other pilot and inviting the child to develop the next stage of the story. This style of parenting can require quick thinking and slow acting rather than getting caught up in the child's tendency to frenetic actions and multiple crashes. Getting the child to rescue your pilot might also be a scenario you could invite once you have modelled it for the child.

Try to avoid getting irritable with your child. Careful use of reward programmes and trouble-shooting the inevitable difficulties that will arise is another important component of behaviour therapy. The guidance of a skilled professional is very helpful here. The treatment can appear obvious but this can be deceptive and the pitfalls are many. Pure behaviour therapy is more likely to be applied through work with the parents or carers and to be aimed at the younger child. For the older child, parallel cognitive behaviour therapy is more useful.

4) Cognitive behaviour therapy (CBT)

Cognitive behaviour therapy with the child or young person can be offered in a group format, e.g. *Dinosaur School*, developed by Webster-Stratton (see www.incredibleyears.com/) or individually or in parallel work with the child and parent, e.g. Stop Think Do (www.stopthinkdo.com/). Each of these models critically depends on the adults in the child's life – principally parents and teachers – understanding how the model works, what stage the child has reached in working with it, and supporting the child's efforts in a non-judgemental fashion.

5) Anger management

Anger management work is also likely to be a useful component of treatment for ADHD if the child has problems controlling his or her temper. Teaching the child to recognise the cues of their anger build-up, before they explode, can be difficult. The child may not be able to categorise emotions, and the explosion can come with little apparent premonition. However, the child can be helped to recognise physiological signs, e.g. heart rate, breathing, sweating, feeling tense. The importance of doing so is that it gives the child more time to problem solve through thinking about possible solutions, the likely consequences and to choose a "good" solution – one that is safe for all concerned and that will have a better chance of leading to the outcome the child desires. The process needs to be worked on in situations that gradually resemble the real-life situations that the child has to manage day to day.

Programmes like *Dinosaur School* combine these different approaches in creative ways that have an evidence base for their effectiveness. This does not mean that they are a cure-all, and the principles may well have to be revisited from time to time in a developmentally sensitive manner.

A more detailed account with references to the evidence base for this work can be found in Sinclair, 2007.

SECTION 1

Medication

Stimulants

Methylphenidate (MPD) is an effective medication that reduces hyperactivity in about 70 per cent of young people who take it. Dexamphetamine is effective in about the same proportion but the two drugs do not necessarily work with the same young people, so that if one is ineffective, it is worth trying the other.

These two main medicines used to treat ADHD and hyperkinetic disorder are both so-called stimulants. They act on catecholamine transmitter systems in the brain. These medicines are scheduled medications (drugs that can be abused) because they can be misused by teenagers and young adults to give a "high" and to counteract sleepiness. However, in hyperactive children and adolescents they do not seem to have this effect; rather, they improve attention and concentration and reduce motor hyperactivity. Clinicians will be reluctant to prescribe these medicines for young people who have a history of abusing substances. It can still be appropriate to do so, but it needs to be carefully monitored in these circumstances. The main risks are that the young person will sell their medication on the street to obtain money for other drugs, or that they will mix their medication with a cocktail of other non-prescribed drugs with the risk of unexpected side-effects.

There is substantial evidence that MPD is effective as a treatment for ADHD and hyperkinetic disorder in the short term. NICE reviewed 49 trials with 7,500 participants published between 1976 and 2007. After careful review of the studies, they concluded that MPD has a medium-to-large effect in reducing ADHD symptoms and conduct problems in school-aged children (NICE, 2008, p254). Some quote the three-year results of a large trial in the US (known as the MTA trial) as evidence that MPD is not effective. This is not the case because the MTA trial ceased delivering and controlling the different treatment packages after 14 months, so that the subsequent follow-up is a naturalistic study, and it is unsurprising that the groups offered different treatments converge – this is discussed and referenced in NICE (2008, section 10.6.4, p 250).

However, the evidence for the long-term effectiveness of MPD is less clear. Anecdotally, some young people stop taking medication during adolescence because they do not think that it is worthwhile, whilst others find it essential to help them concentrate on their schoolwork.

The acute side effects of the stimulants can include irritability, tearfulness (which can be alarming for parents but which usually passes in a day or two if it occurs), abdominal pain, headache and suppression of appetite. These can usually be addressed by lowering the dose for a period of days or, in the case of acute appetite suppression, taking the tablets after breakfast. Other possible side effects are listed below.

- Most children experience some loss of appetite during the day that can concern parents. Usually, they will eat voraciously as the medication wears off or in the evening.

- Sleeplessness is a problem that often accompanies ADHD. It can be made worse by stimulant medication. Sometimes adjusting the amount or timing of doses can help, or using an alternative medicine in the late afternoon or evening. In some cases, a small additional dose of MPD works because the cause of the sleeplessness may be the medication wearing off with some rebound effect.

- Stimulant medication has a small effect on growth. However, it is uncertain whether adult height is reduced or not (Poulton, 2006). The risk may be minimised by ensuring regular drug breaks during the

19

school holidays. Some advocate drug holidays each weekend, but this can lead to a degree of instability for some children because of the body's reaction to switching between taking and stopping medication so regularly.

● There have been rare reports of death associated with taking stimulant medication. However, there is no substantive risk for children who do not have significant heart disease, and even in those cases it may be possible to take the medication provided it is covered by medicine to prevent abnormal heart rhythms developing. This should be monitored by a paediatric cardiologist.

● Black male young people may be at greater risk of a mild elevation in blood pressure, so parents or carers may need to be alert to this. In any event, blood pressure should be monitored regularly (about every three–six months if it is stable and more frequently if there is any concern). Weight and height should be checked at six-monthly intervals. Blood tests are unnecessary.

● Occasionally, stimulants can result in mood changes, which are transient, or depression, which may require lowering the dose of the stimulant or changing to another medication. The clinician will check for signs of depression, tics and irritability at each visit.

● Sometimes stimulants in excess can lead to a reduction in spontaneity – parents tend to describe this as a "zombie state". A reduction in the dose taken by the child is usually sufficient to deal with this. Sometimes it requires a change to an alternative medicine.

- There have been repeated concerns about over-prescription of stimulant medication for children and young people (Jensen et al, 1999; Safer, 2000).

The original forms of MPD and dexamphetamine have a short period of action of three–four hours, so they need to be taken before breakfast and at lunch to have an effect during afternoon schooling. In recent years, long-acting versions of these stimulants have been formulated. For the most part, these allow children to take the medication once daily. This single dose may need to be supplemented by a small dose of short-acting medicine in the morning or late afternoon, depending on the individual child's difficulties.

Non-stimulant medication

None of the other medicines used to treat ADHD are as effective as the stimulants described above. However, several medicines have useful action in the treatment of ADHD.

Most recently these include Atomoxetine, which takes a few weeks before noticeable effects are seen in the child's behaviour. You may start to see changes in about three weeks, but it can be two months before the full effect of a prescribed dose can be assessed. The disadvantage of this is that it can take much longer to achieve the best dose for a particular child. The advantage of using this medicine is that it avoids the use of a controlled drug. But a statistically significant increase in the rate of suicidal ideas has been found in children taking this medicine and clinicians should monitor this carefully. More commonly, abdominal pain, a dry mouth, irritability or nausea occur as side effects.

Other medications used to treat ADHD include the tricyclic antidepressants imipramine and despramine. The main disadvantage of these medicines is that they can be dangerous in overdose to children and young people especially, because they can cause cardiac dysrhythmias (irregular heartbeat and pumping difficulties). They are effective but less so than the stimulants.

Clonidine can be a helpful adjunct in the treatment of hyperactivity. However, it does not seem to help concentration, and can cause difficulties with low blood pressure or rebound of high blood pressure if it is stopped abruptly. It can be helpful to combat anxiety that accompanies ADHD in a proportion of cases. Occasionally it can lead to depression.

A promising medicine will be appearing in the next year or two: guanfacine hydrochloride. This has been used in the US for a number of years but has not yet been available in the UK.

There are other medications that are used as second-line drugs. They include bupropion, risperidone, modafinil and nicotine patches. Any of the non-stimulant medicines may be useful if the first-line medicines are ineffective or have to be stopped because of side effects. Habituation to particular medicines can occur. This may need an increased dose or changing to another medicine, either temporarily or permanently.

It is always a reasonable request to ask for a factsheet about a medicine and to have a detailed discussion with the doctor who is hoping to prescribe it.

Prognosis for ADHD

This varies according to age, accompanying difficulties and the environment (Taylor and Sonuga-Barke, 2008). Poor regulation of attention and activity are quite common in infancy, but if this still persists by the age of four, it is likely to persist into the school years (Lahey *et al*, 2004). Approximately half of the children developing ADHD by school age will carry the disorder into adolescence (Klein and Mannuzza, 1991). The NICE guideline suggests that about 15 per cent of adults retain the diagnosis of ADHD at the age of 25 years. However, 65 per cent of childhood sufferers will be in partial remission in adulthood with some associated symptoms and some impairment of their everyday function (NICE, 2008, p108).

If your child shows overactivity and impulsiveness rather than solely inattention, there is a significant risk that he or she will develop aggressive and anti-social behaviour and that he or she may later develop delinquency (Farrington, 1995; Sibley et al, 2011). However, this is by no means inevitable.

There is also an increased likelihood of substance misuse in adolescence. This is not related to the use of stimulant medication to treat the ADHD as the risk is reduced in those who take stimulants (Wilens et al, 2003).

SECTION 1

23

CHAPTER **3**

Frequently asked questions

Isn't it all bad parenting and attachment disorder really?

No. There are strong genetic links to ADHD. There are things that mothers may have done during pregnancy that increase the likelihood of the child developing ADHD, including use of cocaine, heroin, certain medicines and alcohol misuse. Smoking in pregnancy is another probable factor. Severe and prolonged (longer than six months) neglect, as seen in some children who were raised in Romanian orphanages, is associated with persistent symptoms of inattention and impulsivity.

What do children say about what ADHD feels like?

Children often like the "buzzy feel" and sense of energy that they have with ADHD. Sometimes children dislike taking medication as it takes away this feeling even though it helps them to concentrate. They yearn for friends but do not understand that they do things that put most other children off. They often feel that life is unfair and behave as if it is other children who are at fault rather than themselves.

What is the difference between ADHD and ADD?

Some children have the disorder with predominating symptoms of inattention, but without the motor hyperactivity and impulsivity (or they have these to a markedly lesser extent). In the US classification, these children are treated as a separate sub-type (ADD) of ADHD.

Why is my child labelled as having "hyperkinetic conduct disorder"?

This can feel unhelpful to parents. The category exists in the diagnostic scheme to describe the relatively common situation where a child shows signs of both ADHD and serious conduct problems. Each of these behaviours needs treatment in their own right. If both types of behaviour are present, the prognosis tends to be worse without vigorous intervention to address the conduct.

Why are some children hyperactive in one situation but not in others?

We do not really understand the complete reasons for this. Contributions seem to include the importance and interest that a particular activity has for the child; that, of course, may not

25

correspond with how important the adults regard the activity. Children can be a challenge at home but not in school and the other way around, for reasons well summarised in Taylor (2007, p 13):

- The child's behaviour is the same across situations but the responses of the adults differ.

- The impact of the behaviour differs across situations, e.g. wandering may be very disruptive in a classroom but not at home.

- One situation impacts on the other, e.g. a child may hold things together during the school day only to explode when they arrive home.

- There is an interaction between the child and a particular situation. Interestingly, this may arise from genetic reasons as well as reasons to do with the specific environment.

Example

A child may reveal difficulty with learning by disruptive or hyperactive behaviour when they are being presented with tasks that are at or beyond the limit of what they feel they can comfortably achieve. A child subjected to disorganisation or to criticism at home, which they do not experience in school, may feel stressed and react adversely.

What happens in an assessment for ADHD?

The assessment is likely to be led by a child psychiatrist or a paediatrician. It will often involve others such as a community psychiatric nurse, clinical psychologist or speech and language therapist and, occasionally, an occupational therapist. It may take place over a few sessions. One purpose of an assessment is to better understand whether the ADHD is occurring alongside other difficulties such as conduct problems or anxiety; whether the hyperactivity is part of an autism spectrum disorder; or whether learning difficulties are playing a part in the presentation.

Often, parents/carers and teachers are asked to complete questionnaires ahead of the first interview. These are used to gather different views about the child and the impact of the difficulties on the child's life, and will alert clinicians to the range of diagnoses they should consider. The family may well be invited to bring along other children living at home, as they could have valuable perspectives to share that might lead to specific pieces of work between siblings or with the whole family.

The child may be seen by a clinical psychologist to assess whether there is a generalised or specific learning difficulty, and to measure the ability of the child to inhibit their impulsivity or to sustain their attention on boring tasks. A carefully designed assessment can help in advising teachers and others on appropriate interventions and ways to present school material that is more likely to be successful for that particular child. The child will usually have an individual interview to hear their point of view, to understand if there are any other factors at play that the child has not mentioned to others, e.g. bullying, and to talk about the type of interventions that might be most appropriate for this child and family.

After feedback, a treatment plan will be discussed with the parents or carers and, depending on age and understanding, with the child.

SECTION I

Are there any tests for ADHD?

No, but sometimes the doctor will recommend that some blood investigations are done to exclude other known medical conditions that are associated with the child having ADHD, e.g. a blood test to exclude Fragile-X syndrome.

What are "comorbid disorders"?

Quite commonly, child mental health disorders occur together, and ADHD is no different in this respect. Sometimes the other disorder is causal for the hyperactivity; more commonly, the two disorders co-occur and there is no evidence that the other disorder is the root cause of the hyperactivity. It is known that hyperactivity can be found with:

- oppositional defiant disorder

- conduct disorder

- anxiety disorders

- learning disability

- autism spectrum disorders

- Tourette syndrome

- substance use disorders

This does not mean that a child who has ADHD also has, or is inevitably going to develop, one of these disorders. It does mean that they are at higher risk of doing so than children who do not have ADHD.

In recent times, clinicians have increasingly recognised the overlap in some young people of ADHD with milder forms of the autism spectrum. Quite what the origin of this is remains unclear at present. We increasingly see some young children who present clinically as having ADHD in their behavioural style and who, on re-evaluation at around the age of 11, are also found to have an autism spectrum presentation. This does not apply to most children with ADHD, but if major difficulties are anticipated or experienced at secondary school transfer, it may be a signal to undertake further assessment.

How can we choose the right treatment?

The most appropriate treatments depend on the age of the child and the severity of the disorder. A group-based training/education programme for the treatment and management of conduct disordered children should be offered to parents and carers of all children with ADHD, whether or not they have a diagnosis of conduct disorder.

Individual training/educational programmes should be offered to the parents or carers if there are special reasons to do so, such as language differences that may preclude a parent from accessing a group training/education programme.

All programmes are intended to educate the parents or carers of the child about ADHD and/or conduct disorder, but also to focus on building their skills to manage the difficult behaviour of their child.

Parents or carers may want to look for programmes that meet as many as possible of the following criteria. The programme should:

● be structured and have a curriculum informed by principles of social learning theory;

- include relationship-enhancing strategies;

- offer a sufficient number of sessions, with an optimum of 8–12, to maximise the possible benefits for participants;

- enable parents to identify their own parenting objectives;

- incorporate role-play during sessions, as well as homework to be undertaken between sessions, to achieve application of newly rehearsed skills to the home situation;

- be delivered by appropriately trained and skilled facilitators who are supervised, have access to necessary ongoing professional development, and are able to engage in a productive therapeutic alliance with parents;

- adhere to the programme developer's manual and employ all of the necessary materials to ensure consistent implementation of the programme (NICE and SCIE, 2006).

For the school-aged child, parent/carer group work as above should be combined with CBT directly with the child. This may be delivered in group or individual format. It should target a number of areas such as social skills with peers, social problem solving, self-control, listening skills, and learning to recognise and express feelings in a safe way. Active learning strategies should form the core approach so that homework can be undertaken by the child with the help of their parents or carers. Rewards for achievement are a useful tool in this approach. They do not have to be material rewards – they could be activities with parents or carers that do not have to be expensive.

For adolescents, an individual CBT approach may be more

acceptable, keeping parents or carers informed and involving them as appropriate.

Careful review of all children should take place periodically to ensure that any other coexisting difficulties, such as anxiety, learning difficulties, etc, are addressed.

For children with more severe ADHD (hyperkinetic disorder), medication is likely to be an important component of treatment, but it should not be the only treatment mobilised.

As the NICE guideline points out (2008), you will help your child if you think about life stresses, such as a change of school, puberty, etc, ahead of time so that you can develop a plan with your clinician to help your child through the transition.

Do special diets work?

Two sorts of alterations to diet have been tried: supplementing the diet with substances that are supposed to be lacking; or eliminating substances that are thought to be toxic. Diets including supplements have mainly focused on giving additional long chain fatty acids, as it has been thought that these may be lacking in the brains of children with ADHD. To date, no convincing evidence of the effectiveness of adding polyunsaturated fats to the diet of children with ADHD has been produced. One study seems to show positive effects at home, but this was not recognised in school (Sinn and Bryan, 2007). Until more convincing evidence is produced, the NICE recommendation of not using these supplements stands (2008, p 230). Other trials are still being carried out.

Various dietary restrictions have been tried with children who have ADHD. There was a lot of parent support in the past for the Feingold diet, eliminating artificial food additives and salicylates.

This was rather restrictive, and no substantive, consistent evidence for its effectiveness has been produced. Subsequently, there have been two open trials: the open phase identified substances that the parents thought affected their child's behaviour when they were introduced; this was followed by a double blind design, in which the substances were added or removed in a way that neither the investigator nor the family could tell at the time (Egger et al, 1985; Carter et al, 1993). These trials have suggested that parents can indeed recognise the particular food(s) that affect their children idiosyncratically. Foods identified included cow's milk, citrus, wheat, eggs as well as artificial colouring and additives (NICE, 2008, p 228).

Overall, there is some, if limited, evidence to show that foods can affect the behaviour of children with a diagnosis of ADHD and probably other children too. However, adjusting a child's diet to eliminate particular foods is often a large undertaking that has a significant impact on the child's life in addition to the effect that is sought.

CHAPTER 4

Specific parenting tasks

Children with ADHD can be difficult to parent. Sometimes this is variable and there will be good times. Sometimes it can feel relentless. The child's difficulty with concentration and impulsiveness can lead to low self-esteem. It is easy to get into a negative mindset with your child in these circumstances. Criticism and hostility, antagonism and negativity and low responsiveness to the child are often a feature in the birth families of children with ADHD. Unfortunately, ADHD can evoke the same response in adoptive and foster families because these children do exasperating things. It has been shown that critical parenting does harm to the development of children, including those with ADHD. Fortunately, treatment with methylphenidate and appropriate parenting training can improve this situation (Schachar *et al*, 1997).

- Children with ADHD need their parents or carers to be skilled in behavioural management. They need them to be able to adapt their skills over time as the child grows up and enters adolescence.

- They need their parents/carers to teach them how to negotiate; how to give and take.

- They need support in self-organisation, which they often find very difficult.

- They may well have some learning difficulties as well as ADHD and will need support with reading and homework. This can be very hard for parents or carers, as the child may be avoidant. At times, it may be more supportive to use after-school homework clubs to avoid conflict with parents/carers.

- Children with ADHD need their parents/carers to be effective advocates on their behalf, and subtle educators to help their teacher to learn about ADHD and the particular difficulties that this child has (as opposed to children with ADHD in general). Parents/ carers and teachers need to become allies: not to "gang up" on the frustrating child, but so that they can work as a team to help the child. Parents/carers and the school will have to consider carefully whether a child needs special support and whether such support can be provided in the school without additional resources.

- Parents or carers will need to get their health professionals to work closely with the school and make sure that the GP and specialist are working together for their child.

- If a child is in foster care, there will be the added complexities of working with social services and sometimes the child's birth family, particularly if one or both of the child's parents themselves have ADHD.

In other words, working as a foster carer or an adoptive parent of a child who has ADHD requires energy, commitment, subtlety, firmness and great negotiating skills! Having said all that, I am repeatedly surprised at how people who never thought they had these attributes find them when they are needed. Being brave enough to talk about the difficult bits with your specialist or to seek a referral to Child and Adolescent Mental Health Services (CAMHS) may be very helpful in thinking through some aspects of what this book describes. As Section II indicates, bringing up a child with ADHD can be very rewarding. It is unlikely to be dull.

SECTION I

CHAPTER **5**

How ADHD might affect a child at different stages of development

The pre-school years

Many children show some hyperactivity in the pre-school years. This is likely to be part of normal brain development, but among these children, there will be some who are developing the ADHD syndrome early. If this pattern is leading to impairment of function compared with the child's same-age peers, then it is appropriate for the parent or carer to be suspicious and to ask their GP for a referral.

If the child has recently moved to your family, then he or she may settle. If the symptoms are still present six months later, then referral for assessment is appropriate. ADHD presenting between the ages of three and five is often accompanied by oppositional behaviour. Occasionally, it is an indication of a more pervasive developmental disorder. In any event, proper assessment, carefully chosen schooling and attending a parenting course may prove helpful. You should not feel that to attend such a course is in any way an admission of failure. Children with ADHD require extra-special parenting to give them the best chance of success and none of us have been trained except through our own experience of being parented.

The primary school years

This is the typical age of presentation for ADHD. The way you work with your child, teachers and others has the potential to minimise the difficulties in the child's teenage years. That does not mean that there is a cure and that there will be no problems, but with careful attention, judicious use of stimulant or other medication as advised, and using parenting techniques consistently, your child is likely to benefit greatly.

However, you do not have to get it right all of the time: nobody does. It is important to find out what resources are available to help you and your child in the area in which you live. There may be support groups for parents or carers. There may even be special activities for children with ADHD that you can access or social skills groups to help your child directly, or courses that will help you to coach your child in developing friendships (Mikami et al, 2010).

The teenage years

This can be a worrying time for the parent or carer of a hyperactive youngster. For any adolescent, it is a time of separating from their parents, of seeking independence and of discovering that they cannot quite manage it; of false starts as well as a time of growth emotionally and socially. Children with ADHD may well struggle with the increased complexity of social

SECTION 1

37

relationships, even more than other young people. If they have developed conduct problems, then it is likely to be these that will cause difficulties in adolescence. There are several good manuals that use a social learning approach to help parents of teenage young people; examples of these include Munden and Arcelus, 1999; Parker, 1999; and Patterson and Forgatch, 2005a, 2005b. All are currently in print.

In general, it is very important to know where your teenage son or daughter is, with whom, and to have agreements about when they will return. The young person with ADHD will be even more prone than other teenagers to forget this. Negotiating freedom with rewards and sanctions is important. Being available for your child to talk to and confide in, without trying to be a "mate", is a real skill. Helping them to slow themselves down enough to weigh decisions, and as far as possible get into the habit of doing so, and steering them away from friends who get them into difficulties are more desirable skills at this stage. Encouraging them to use clubs and activities to develop interests and friendship circles can be another approach.

Finally, remember to be realistic and to enjoy the time you have with your adolescent child. As ever, it is the relationship you have developed that will give you some influence if used positively.

Education

Children with ADHD quickly fail academically, falling progressively behind their peers. There have been problems of under-recognition of ADHD in UK schools. In-service training to help teachers recognise the meaning of the difficult behaviours they see in some children is needed as well as help to learn effective strategies to educate the child.

ADHD affects children's ability to consider alternative information in problem solving – they jump to conclusions. They cannot wait and this leads to poor test performance; they are disorganised and do not read instructions. They tend not to ask for help, especially if this would lead to delay of gratification (for the hyperactive child, the gratification is finishing the task – without regard for their standard of work).

The individual teacher's management of behaviour in the classroom has an important impact on the child with ADHD. Teachers who can evoke a calm atmosphere, have a structured classroom strategy that includes behaviour management, and who can make adaptations for the hyperactive child are likely to be more successful. Cooper and Ideus (1996) suggest useful practical advice for teachers which is quoted in the NICE guideline (2008):

- Seating the child in a place that is relatively free from distraction (for example, doors and windows) in a position where the teacher can easily intervene if the child is not attending.

- Having a designated quiet area for a child to work in.

- Providing stimulating activities.

- Giving concise, clear instructions.

- Following a defined, regular timetable.

- Avoiding repetitive tasks.

- Breaking down tasks into a series of small steps.

- Giving frequent positive feedback.

- Working in a pair rather than a group.

- Isolating the child from the class for a short time when they are misbehaving.

SECTION 1

39

- Giving points or tokens as rewards to be exchanged at a later time for a favourite activity or treat.

- Taking away points or tokens if the child misbehaves.

It may be that removing points and tokens is less effective, and "time out" for a few minutes can be more useful if signposted with matter-of-fact warnings.

Sinclair (2007) points out the importance of good home–school communication to ensure that information does not get distorted. Stressors at home may affect the child's behaviour in school and vice versa. If teachers and families are alerted, they can watch out for changes in behaviour and make allowances for the child's forgetfulness that is part and parcel of the disorder.

Education for teachers about ADHD is vital in helping them to understand the difficulties that these children have and to devise strategies for supporting the pupil. Such teacher training is time consuming and one study suggests that it takes 30 hours of training to achieve sustained changes in classroom practice (Adey et al, 2004). Topics that have been found useful by teachers include:

- knowledge about ADHD;

- adapting lessons for pupils with ADHD;

- managing stress caused by children with ADHD in the classroom;

- behavioural management;

- implementation of behaviour plans (NICE, 2008, p 218).

Training teachers is much more effective if the parents undertake parenting training as well. Some useful advice in liaising with school teachers can be found on the internet, e.g. Block and Smith, 2010; Steer, 2010.

Social issues

The social difficulties seen among children with ADHD are reviewed in the NICE guideline (2008, pp 105–6). Children with ADHD have difficulty making friends and sustaining friendships. In a large trial of psychosocial and medication interventions in the US, over half of the children had difficulties with peer rejection and less than one per cent were popular. The children's difficulties were linked to ADHD and not to other diagnoses that might also be present. They occurred in boys and girls of all ages (Hoza *et al*, 2005; Hoza, 2007).

Boys with ADHD seem to like the same peers that other children do when aged seven to nine, but later tend to develop friendships with other children who have difficulties. They do not monitor their own social behaviour well and have poor insight into their own poor performance. Girls with ADHD tend to have fewer friends and more problems with peers and members of the opposite sex.

Conclusion

A child who is placed with you who has ADHD will be a challenge. He or she will have the same needs for love and care as other children. They will need consistent, firm, kind boundaries; you will need an ability to adapt to new situations with humour and tolerance; to know when to give way and when to stand your ground. You will need to learn the child's talents and to help the child learn not to impulsively put his or her own safety at risk. Your child will need to learn to recognise his or her own emotions and to try to be thoughtful about others. These things have to be learned, in spite of the child being held back by finding such things particularly difficult. The child may well thrive on outside activities. He or she needs your support to realise that

SECTION I

they are not a freak, that the condition is common but that it can be helped. Often this will require the use of medication. He or she needs you as an intelligent advocate. The difference these factors can make for many children is humbling.

As so often in fostering and adoption, love of itself is not enough. It is an essential component of that special mix that brings such children to a fulfilling adult life, but it also needs realism, hope, problem-solving skills and an ability on the part of carers and parents to learn new skills at each stage of the child's life. The remarkable thing is that many of us, who as prospective parents doubt whether we have these qualities, grow into them.

PARENTING CHILDREN AFFECTED BY ADHD

LORNA MILES

Lorna Miles is an adoptive parent and has been a foster carer on and off for 25 years. In addition, she has worked with children in care in a variety of settings. In this contribution, Lorna tells of her family's experience of fostering several children with ADHD and/or similar conditions.

'Lively', 'over the top', 'a bit of a handful', 'a busy little chap', 'excitable and always on the go' are phrases that were used to describe some of the children we have fostered since the mid-1980s, and whom we now suspect may have had ADHD. It is easy to be wise in hindsight, but at the time we knew little about what was then generally called hyperactivity or Attention Deficit Disorder. As far as I was aware, there were only two possible causes for this type of behaviour: poor parenting and poor diet. There had been a flurry in the press about children who were being treated for this condition with a drug called Ritalin; nothing I read about this drug was good. Statements like 'worse than cocaine', 'addictive' and, worst case scenario, 'could lead to death through organ failure or suicide', convinced me that no child I cared for would ever be subjected to medication with these possible side effects.

One of the first children we fostered who was hyperactive in the extreme was Rory. He arrived with the police as an emergency placement late one Friday evening, having been left "home alone" by his teenage mum. Having Rory, aged eighteen months, in the house was like living with a whirlwind. He rarely slept and, unless I could give him my undivided attention, needed to be contained in a playpen; otherwise he would dismantle the house within seconds. His climbing skills would have put Sir Edmund Hillary to shame, and even when we were outside the house he would wreak havoc.

On our first shopping trip into town I thought that as he was securely fastened in the pushchair he couldn't get up to any mischief. How wrong I was! As I returned to my car and took the rain cover off the pushchair, I discovered that it had been concealing a collection of "goodies" which had caught Rory's eye as we had gone from shop to shop. Single shoes and slippers, sweets, a ladies jumper and a toy car had been secreted away without my knowledge. I spent the next hour returning all the items to their respective shops, hoping that my very red face served as confirmation that this hadn't been some kind of fumbled shoplifting attempt.

Given the background information we had on Rory, I believed that his hyperactivity could be attributed to poor parenting. I felt sure that a few weeks of settled routines and a healthy diet was all that would be needed to enable him to calm down. But weeks became months and there was no sign of improvement.

It looked as if Rory would be with us for some time as his future was uncertain, so I decided that I needed to find out more. I had tried to talk to the health visitor about Rory's behaviour but she was very dismissive and implied that I was making a fuss about nothing. But I had cared for enough children to realise that Rory's behaviour was not the norm.

My local bookshops offered nothing on the subject, so I went further afield to an "alternative" bookshop and there I had success. Published some ten years earlier, *Why your Child is Hyperactive*, by Ben F Feingold, seemed to back up the theory that diet was the key. In fact, the frontispiece claimed that 'remarkable personality and behavioural changes' could be brought about 'when cookies, ice cream, fruit punches, hot dogs and dry cereal are taken away'. A second book, *E for Additives: The complete E number guide*, offered a comprehensive list of both the "good" and "bad" additives and promised to guide me through the 'maze of conflicting interests and pitfalls' enabling me to 'shop wisely'. I could hardly wait to get home and start to put the plan into action!

Over the following months I trailed around the supermarkets and health food stores armed with a list of forbidden foods. These mainly consisted of items that were laced with large amounts of artificial colourings and flavourings, such as orange squash, sweets and a

47

whole host of other foods when I read the small print. In fact, having read the books, I had become so concerned about the harm I could have been unknowingly inflicting upon my family that I changed the whole family's diet. Rory's behaviour, however, remained the same!

It was decided that Rory should be placed for adoption, all efforts to enable him to return home having failed. I repeatedly raised the issue of his hyperactivity with all concerned but the response I got was: 'Do you really want him on Ritalin?', as if I were pronouncing a death sentence. All I wanted was some kind of formal, professional assessment – but that was not to be.

After he had been with us for a little over 18 months, Rory, now aged three, was finally placed for adoption with a childless couple; the belief was that as soon as he was "settled", all would be well. We doubted that, but had little say in the matter. I tried to talk to the adoptive couple about my concerns and to share with them some of the strategies I had put in place, but they too were dismissive, claiming that the past was the past, and that once he started a "new life" and knew that he was loved, he would respond accordingly.

It was with huge sadness that, about a year later, we learned that the adoption had broken down and that Rory was, once more, in foster care.

Rory had sparked my interest in ADD, or ADHD as it later became known, and I tried to keep abreast of current thinking on the subject. But it wasn't until the early 2000s when we were taking a break from fostering to support our twin sons, David and Malcolm, through the "exam years" that I met a young man who really made me think about the "Ritalin debate" again. Johnny was 15 and one of my students when I was working as a Basic Skills tutor in a Youth Offenders Institute. He was tall, lean and stalked around the classroom with all the agility and stealth of a big cat.

His behaviour was unpredictable and he was often confined to his cell, where I would work with him one-to-one. In this situation he started to open up about his past; he said that he had ADHD and that his mum couldn't cope with him so he had been in care since the age of seven. His educational history was chequered to say the least, but he could recall a time when he had been taking Ritalin and for the first time had felt like he could focus. He described it as a fog being lifted, of being able to think before he acted, and he appeared to remember it as a time of hope.

For reasons he didn't know or understand, the medication had stopped when he was 12 and that was when he started to slide down a slippery slope into a life of crime. He began to take illegal drugs to try and replicate the feeling that the Ritalin had induced and took increasing amounts or even stronger drugs when they didn't have the desired effect. He was currently incarcerated for TWOC (Taking [a car] without owner's consent) and was on a drugs rehabilitation programme. Johnny was a likeable lad and was realistic about the little hope he had of getting back into education or of ever getting a job when he was "on the out". He found prison life psychologically painful because of the physical containment and his need to be constantly on the move. This was something other inmates who spoke to me about ADHD also commented on: how any situation which made them feel "trapped" made their symptoms worse, like someone was screaming 'get out!' inside their head. Even sitting in the classroom where they knew they had to stay for a certain period of time was unbearable.

One of the privileges for good behaviour in the institute was a television set, and again Johnny was not alone in saying that watching the moving image on the screen gave him some kind of inner peace: although he wasn't physically moving, his body and mind responded as if he were.

I was making good progress with Johnny; I was starting to understand how he "ticked". I didn't impose a rule of sitting down in my classroom: often lads lay on the floor, or wrote standing up with their book resting against the wall. But they were engaged and learning, which was what mattered to me.

One day, Johnny arrived late for class; he came into the room but his usual lithe movements had become heavy and aggressive. He pulled chairs in and out, banged the table and snarled at everyone in the room. I tried to engage with him but he rounded on me, saying 'You're all the f****** same, you don't want me really.' Before I could respond he had up-turned the metal framed table, ripped off the leg and had me pinned to the wall, with the jagged metal table leg pushed against my throat. His dark eyes seared into mine and I could barely find the courage to fumble at my belt for my personal alarm. He seemed oblivious to the demands from the other lads in the group to leave me alone. Eventually he was hauled off by four burly prison officers and I was left badly shaken.

I later found out that Johnny had received a phone call telling him that his foster carers were no longer willing to have him back when he was released. I questioned the wisdom of expecting him to be able to come and join my lesson after receiving such devastating news, but it seemed that deviation from the routine of the "prison day" wasn't allowed in any circumstances.

I spent the next couple of weeks on sick leave recovering from my ordeal, and much of the time I reflected on Johnny's situation. How much of his current circumstances were due to the ADHD itself? Had the withdrawal of the Ritalin played a part or was the fact that it had been prescribed in the first place the root of the problem? I never got the chance to ask Johnny what he thought; when I returned to work I discovered that sadly he had been "shipped off" elsewhere.

By the autumn of 2004, my husband Tim and I had decided that the time was right to return to fostering. We had heard about a therapeutic fostering scheme which had been set up to provide an alternative to residential care for the 2.5 per cent most damaged young people in the care of a neighbouring local authority. This seemed to be just the challenge we were looking for. The day-to-day care of children placed under the scheme was based on principles that promote secure attachments, and so the rigorous assessment process included exploring our own attachments. We needed to be able to respond to the child's needs appropriately even at the most critical of times.

Early in 2005 we were approved and matched with Wayne, aged nine, who we were told had major attachment issues and very challenging behaviour. He was the second eldest of five children; his mother had learning difficulties and suffered from depression. The

51

care of her children had also been adversely affected by her choice of partners. The children had witnessed drug and alcohol misuse and lived in an environment where there were often incidents of extreme domestic violence. The older two boys had frequently been left to look after the younger ones and a "dog-eat-dog" relationship had developed between the siblings. It had been decided that if the children were to have any hope of recovery, they would be better placed as individuals rather than a family group. The three younger children had all been placed for adoption, but Wayne and his older brother Sam, aged 10, remained in care. Sam was with a family a considerable distance away and had contact with Wayne roughly every six weeks. Wayne had been with his current foster carers for about two years, but the placement was at breaking point and a planning meeting was quickly convened to draw up an agreed strategy for Wayne's move to us.

When we met with the carers, they described a lad who was hyperactive, impulsive and disorganised. They were convinced that Wayne had ADHD and were exhausted by his frequent outbursts of temper and an almost constant string of exclusions from school. Wayne had no friends; in fact, children in the locality and their parents actively avoided him whenever they could. He wasn't intentionally unkind or nasty but he had no idea about social cues and just blundered in regardless of who or what was in his way.

As I had done with Rory, nearly 20 years earlier, the carers had made a number of changes to Wayne's diet to try and improve things and we were given a list of "forbidden" foods: coca cola, citrus fruit and drinks, grapes, cow's milk, cheese and more. They were clearly

very fond of Wayne and had done the best they could to
manage him, but they were worn out and demoralised
and, despite having successfully raised three children
of their own, described themselves as having failed. In
some respects Tim and I were really uncomfortable
meeting them, as it felt as if we were being presented
as some kind of "super carers" who would succeed
where they had failed. What made it worse was that
this was their first fostering placement and we couldn't
help but wonder if they would decide that it would
be their last. The truth was that they had been given
very little support by their fostering agency, whereas a
support package was part of our therapeutic foster care
scheme. This included increased social worker contact,
access to a psychologist and a therapist attached to the
local specialist support service for children in care and
adopted children, and regular respite breaks.

It was agreed that after a series of introductions and
overnight stays, Wayne would move to us at the start
of the school Easter holidays. This would give him some
time to settle with us before the start of the new term
when he would have a place at the specialist behavioural
unit of a primary school about eight miles away.

Deciding which school would be best for Wayne had
been a difficult task. The school in our village provided
a small nurturing environment, which could have suited
Wayne well. However, Wayne's current school was
very similar to this and his total inability to refrain
from prodding and poking his classmates and generally
interfering in every aspect of classroom life meant that
he was being educated in the corridor by two teaching
assistants. His boisterous, over the top behaviour also
meant that he was excluded from the playground

SECTION II

53

when the other children had their breaks and he had to take his breaks separately. I had a chat about Wayne with the Head of our local school and although on the surface she seemed encouraging, I detected uneasiness and some apprehension about her welcoming Wayne into her officially rated "Outstanding" domain. She said that Wayne's year group was full and that anyway I would have to apply to the local authority for special permission for him to join the school. After some thought and discussion with Wayne's "team", we decided that he could quickly end up in the corridor again, and in addition get a "bad name" which could prove to be a barrier to him making friendships in the village. The behavioural unit seemed like the best option.

Within days of Wayne's arrival, our home resembled some kind of disaster zone. You always knew where he was because of the trail of destruction he left behind: furniture displaced, muddy hand and foot prints on every available surface and the noise of his constant chatter, regardless of whether anyone was listening or not. Whenever Wayne moved around, his focus was on the final goal, not the obstacles he might encounter en route, so that he was always covered in bruises and bumps. He had several near misses, catching his face or eye on tree branches as he dashed around; our regular visits to get him patched up resulted in us being on first name terms with some of the staff at our local community hospital.

His insatiable need for attention was exhausting, but he was a really delightful lad who was always full of bright ideas, passionate about anything mechanical and was a whizz with technology. He could get a new mobile phone, DVD player, digital camera or any other electronic device up and running before the rest of us had even taken the instructions out of the box!

We tried to use this skill and passion for assembling and "fixing" things as a means to help him be calmer and more focused, and bought him some Airfix car kits. These, of course, not only had to be assembled, but painted as well, and we thought it would give us some respite from Wayne's continuous need to be "on the go". Things got off to a good start, but any interruption to Wayne's concentration was disastrous, because his dreadful memory meant that he couldn't pick up where he had left off and the whole project would be at risk of failing. He also needed constant reassurance that he was doing well, and if left unsupervised for more than a moment or two just couldn't keep "on task" and would lose motivation, down tools and drift off, leaving spilt paint, glue and half-assembled pieces in a trail behind him.

Trying to direct Wayne's energy towards sporting activities was another strategy we tried. First we enrolled him in the local under-11s football team. After a few training sessions he was picked for the team in an under-11s league match. He roared around the pitch, regardless of other players and deaf to the referee's whistle. Tim and I were just discussing what a mistake it had been, when Wayne took control of the ball and started to weave a path to the goal. The rest of his team were shouting 'Wayne, Wayne!' He took a huge kick and deftly planted the ball in the net. It wasn't until a large groan came from the other parents on our side of the pitch that we realised that Wayne had scored an own goal…He wasn't invited to play again. Like so many children who come into the care system, he had missed out on learning the basics of sports at a much younger age and found it difficult to fit in because the grouping was dictated by age not ability. Tag rugby was another sport we explored, having found a mixed age and ability group, but the "tagging" triggered memories of past abuse and Wayne would round aggressively on the other player; it just wasn't safe for him to continue.

Next came swimming, and having negotiated funding for one-to-one swimming lessons because we knew Wayne would never be able to wait his turn as part of a larger group, he literally took to the sport like a "fish to water". He raced through his grades and water skills badges, but trying to take him swimming as a family activity was impossible. He would jump off the side of the pool regardless of whom he might injure and had no concept of why people were annoyed by the tidal wave he created or the litres of water he splashed over them as he frantically swam around. He saw it as everyone else's responsibility to move out of his way, not his responsibility to ensure he had a clear path.

A friend had suggested that trampolining might be a good way to burn off energy, so we took Wayne to the local sports centre to give it a try. He was really good at it and picked up the moves quickly. Again, being part of a group wasn't an option, but after discussion with Wayne's team it was agreed that we would buy a trampoline and safety net for the garden. Wayne loved it and would come home from school and bounce whenever the weather allowed. I also found that a "secret bounce" when no one else was around was a brilliant way for me to deal with the stresses and strains that living with Wayne was producing.

One of the things we had been told about Wayne was that he loved animals. That was clearly true because he immediately started to form a relationship with our two dogs, Holly and Flynn. Flynn, an elderly springer spaniel, took Wayne's arrival in his stride; he was used to a house full of children and was partially deaf too, so probably didn't hear the additional hubbub and noise Wayne was creating. But Holly, a labrador/springer spaniel cross, was only six months old and was as boisterous and lively as Wayne himself. The pair quickly became partners in crime and wherever one went the other was never far behind. It was lovely to see this relationship developing, but, as with all areas of Wayne's life, he didn't know when enough was enough. He would, for example, repeatedly throw a ball for Holly to "fetch": back and forth, back and forth, back and forth she would go before she would flop down on the grass, clearly having had enough. But Wayne just didn't get it. He would wave the ball around in front of her, attempt to haul her to her feet and run back and forth himself trying to get her to move. If she came back into the house to lie in her basket, he would follow to persuade her to go into the garden again. There was no way that I could leave Wayne and the dogs unsupervised, not even for long enough to go to the toilet! So the dogs found themselves shut away in the back porch, where I could hear from the downstairs toilet if Wayne went to let them out whilst I was otherwise engaged.

David and Malcolm, our twin sons, were also on the receiving end of Wayne's relentless drive for attention. Although they were 11 years older than him, they were happy to spend some time with Wayne, listening to music, watching DVDs, going out on their bikes and generally being "older brothers". But Wayne had no understanding of their need for privacy and time alone. Our safer caring policy clearly said that we would knock before going into other peoples' bedrooms; we wouldn't

go in if they were not there and we wouldn't touch other peoples' belongings without their permission. But of course none of this applied to Wayne! Both David and Malcolm are musicians, playing in working bands, so had some very expensive instruments and equipment in their rooms. Wayne would frequently go into their rooms looking for who knows what when they weren't there. Understandably they were worried that their things would be damaged, so we reluctantly had to put locks on their doors. We had never excluded a child in this way before, and although we could see
the need for it, and our fostering agency supported us, it didn't feel right.

We had already discovered that working to a fairly strict timetable and predictable routine was helping Wayne's hyperactive behaviour, but by thinking things through a little more carefully we could also make things less stressful for ourselves. It had quickly become apparent that although we had expected previous foster children to adapt to our routine after a reasonable period of time, with Wayne we were going, to a certain extent, to have to adapt our routines to fit his behaviour. Again, this didn't feel entirely comfortable because it felt like Wayne was controlling us, but seemed worth it if it saved everyone's sanity.

The only time when Wayne was reasonably calm was when he was watching TV and whilst we didn't agree with using it as a "babysitter", there were occasions when allowing him to watch a favourite programme or a DVD ensured that he was as safe as he could be while I was doing other essential things and couldn't give him my undivided attention.

If Wayne was at a friend's house and I needed things from the local shop, getting them on my way to collect Wayne rather than on the way back avoided him touching everything in sight and me forgetting half the things I needed in my efforts to stop him. If I bumped into a friend when out with Wayne, it was better to arrange to ring her later or meet again the following day when Wayne was at school, rather than expect Wayne to wait patiently whilst I had a conversation. I had to accept what he just couldn't do, and that I would only be making my life more stressful by trying to force him. Of course, having rules for Wayne which were different from those David and Malcolm were used to caused controversy. 'You would have never let me get away with that…I wouldn't have dared try that one…are you going soft?' became familiar cries. Of course, they were of an age where we could sit and talk things through with them and help them understand, but if you have younger children, this apparent inconsistency in your expectations of behaviour must be incredibly difficult to manage.

Wayne never slept in beyond 5am, and if we were lucky we might have managed five hours of sleep by then. Taking a bath, a warm milky drink, bedtime stories and any other strategy we tried to help Wayne unwind before bed all failed. We bought a roller blind to use in addition to the curtains to try and make the room as dark as possible, but it only served as an additional distraction for Wayne as he pulled it up and down repeatedly. When he did eventually go to sleep, he often woke several times through the night because of nightmares, wet beds and reasons unknown. We were functioning on auto-pilot.

Having lived with Wayne for several months, we agreed that he was certainly ticking all the boxes for ADHD.

The psychologist had made an assessment that gave an overall picture of the severity of a child's problems. Wayne scored in the highest bracket. It would have been easy at this point to conclude that Wayne did in fact have ADHD and begin the medication debate. But the psychologist, the community paediatrician and Wayne's social worker were mindful of the fact that children with Wayne's background are often misdiagnosed with ADHD and they didn't want to jump to conclusions.

There was no doubt that Wayne had severe attachment difficulties; he had also experienced multiple traumatic events: witnessing domestic violence, living in inappropriate housing or on the streets, being removed from his birth family and then separated from his siblings as one by one they were placed for adoption. As a result, a diagnosis of complex developmental trauma was also a strong possibility. Both these conditions could result in symptoms that mimic ADHD.

Attachment-disordered children are often chronically over-aroused in association with having been traumatised and inconsistently soothed in their primary-dependency relationships…They are more prone than other children to aggressive, destructive, hyperactive and dissociative behaviours…Children who behave like this are often misdiagnosed with Attention Deficit Hyperactivity Disorder.

(Levine and Kline, 2007, pp 39–43)

Prolonged exposure to a stressful environment leads to numbing and shutdown as the fear and pain become increasingly unbearable. This develops into lifelong patterns that are commonly (mis-)diagnosed years later (usually when the child begins school) as Anxiety Disorder, Attention Deficit Disorder, Hyperactivity.

(Levine and Kline, 2007, p 34)

Overall, things at school were going well, there had been a few "blips" but the structure and routine of the unit, the high ratio of staff to pupils and an excellent home–school relationship meant that, for the first time in his academic history, Wayne was enjoying a positive experience of school life. Taking all of this into account, it was decided to put exploring the options available for the "treatment" of ADHD on hold, and hope that as Wayne started to recover, things would improve.

I had tried, one by one, including and excluding the foods Wayne's previous carers had identified as exacerbating his problems, and with the exception of coca-cola, had found they made no difference. Even with coca-cola, I had found that just one glass didn't really make much difference, but an evening of repeated drinks increased his hyperactivity, so I suspected that the high sugar levels were responsible. I had heard some alarming reports about the products that were being used as a sugar alternative to sweeten children's drinks and so continued to use the sugared varieties but kept them as occasional treats.

At first, clashes with Wayne's social worker over various

parenting strategies which the attachment-focused re-parenting project required, and lack of suitable respite carers, coupled with what could be labelled Wayne's ADHD behaviour, were an exhausting combination. On more than one occasion Tim and I felt that we just couldn't go on. Wayne's demands were relentless and way above what we had envisaged when we had agreed to take him on. But a year into the placement, and with regular respite finally in place, things became just about bearable. Then came a bombshell!

At Wayne's Special Educational Needs Review, just a few weeks before the end of the summer term in 2006, the school announced that as the unit Wayne was attending was for children with behavioural problems, and as Wayne's behaviour had improved so much, he no longer met the criteria to remain in the unit. All of Wayne's team raised concerns about the impact this could have on him and the possible risk of regression, but there was a long waiting list for places and our pleas for the decision to be reconsidered fell on deaf ears.

Despite having been reasonably settled in the unit, Wayne had failed to make any significant progress in literacy and numeracy, and it was felt that he might have underlying learning difficulties which, due to his lack of co-operation, had not been assessed. It was therefore decided that he should move to a nearby school for children with learning difficulties, called Rosefield. Everything was done in such a rush that there was no time for them to assess Wayne properly and identify what support he would need. He was to move from the nurturing environment of the unit to a class of 20 children all with special needs and with no designated teaching assistant.

Almost as soon as the new academic year started, things began to go wrong. I had asked for someone to meet Wayne from his taxi and make sure he went into school safely as had happened at the unit, but no one was available to fulfil this role, so he was dropped off on the school drive and expected to make his own way into the building. He came home with tales of hiding in the bushes with a group of older lads who were smoking something out of a bag! He climbed and fell out of a tree and sustained a nasty injury to his bottom when he caught it on a catch as he followed another boy climbing through a window…and this was even before the school day had started. Once in the classroom things were no better. His hyper-vigilance and hyperactivity were made worse by the behaviour of the other children in the class; some had difficulties such as Tourette syndrome, autism and other conditions, the nature of which often caused them to respond in an unpredictable manner. If Wayne had been supported by a teaching assistant who could have explained there was nothing to fear, he could probably have adjusted, but there was no provision for this in his Statement of Special Educational Needs.

As the term progressed, Wayne's challenging behaviour escalated and he was being sent home almost daily. I didn't realise at the time, but these "informal" exclusions were, in fact, illegal: either he should have been excluded and I should have received the required paperwork from the Head or Wayne should have been in school. As Christmas approached, Tim and I were in despair; Wayne's behaviour at home was also at a point where it wasn't safe for me to be on my own with him.

As the term drew to an end, I was feeling exhausted and for only the second time in my life became ill

SECTION II

63

with a serious case of the flu. Tim attended the school Christmas production, in which Wayne was supposed to play a snowman. When Tim returned home he was really upset: he described all the children parading into the hall in pairs and then at the rear of the group came Wayne. He was flanked by two members of staff, who were so close to him that he was almost squashed between them. Instead of sitting with the rest of the children, he was directed to sit on a chair on the sidelines, again sandwiched between two members of staff. That was the extent of Wayne's involvement in the play! Tim said that he had felt physically sick as Wayne was paraded into the hall like some criminal going to the gallows. How much longer could this go on?

Christmas was a disaster because Wayne was "off the wall" and in early January I arrived at a prearranged meeting to discuss his progress, in tears. We had decided as a family that we just couldn't go on – either things at school had to change or we would have to give up on the placement. There was much discussion, and of course the subject of ADHD came up again but this time linked with the suggestion that perhaps we should try medication. I felt physically sick: apart from all the bad press these drugs had attracted, and flashbacks of Johnny racing through my mind, I had issues with medication generally. From quite a young age I had experienced allergic reactions to a number of prescribed drugs, in particular, antibiotics. In addition, when my mother developed the autoimmune disease Systemic Lupus Erythematosus in her late forties, she made a conscious decision to take medication, even if the side effects had an impact on her life expectancy, because she had grandchildren she wanted to enjoy, and because she was so debilitated by the condition. Although I fully respected and supported this decision, it seemed to me that the side effects of one drug led to the need for another, and so it went on, until at the time of her death at the age of 57 she was taking over 50 tablets a day. This just reinforced my belief that medication was best avoided.

It was decided that we would remove Wayne from school for a six-week period, to allow him to calm down and to give the school time to appoint a full-time teaching assistant to support him.

Almost as soon as Wayne received this news, things began to improve, and after a week of low-key activities we were able to start the work that the school was sending home for him. But trying to get him to sit at a table to complete the work was a nightmare: he would twitch, fidget, rub his eyes, put his head on the table and generally behave in a way which implied that he found it mentally impossible to be contained in this way. When I started to allow him to complete the work in a place of his choosing, he lay on the floor, stood up or even walked around. In this way we began to make real progress and soon the schoolwork took only a fraction of the day.

As far as possible, given that it was the middle of winter, we tried to spend time each day outdoors, alternating between sitting down to work and being active. We spotted birds, measured the changing depth of the stream, identified trees and looked out for the first signs of spring flowers, not forgetting walking the dogs. One day, when we were in the middle of the woods, Wayne stopped and said, 'Listen!'
As hard as I tried, apart from the birds singing, I couldn't hear a thing. 'Sorry, I can't hear anything.'
'No, that's it, it's so peaceful, and I love it.' Wayne just

SECTION II

65

stood still, absorbing the atmosphere, no fidgeting, no chatter, looking completely relaxed. I thought about Johnny and the other lads I had met in the Youth Offenders Institute and how they had described feelings of being trapped and their heads just "exploding". In their attempts to deal with Wayne's behaviour, Rosefield school had made his world smaller and smaller. He wasn't allowed in the playground at all, he was often contained in a small room next to the classroom and when the rest of the school went swimming or did PE he wasn't allowed to join in and was expected to do literacy and numeracy work instead. I could understand why his challenging behaviour had escalated.

A friend in the US had introduced me to the work of Richard Louv, author of *Last Child in the Woods: Saving our children from Nature-Deficit Disorder* (2005). Louv claims that there is a direct link between the more sedentary, indoor lifestyles our children lead today and an increase in childhood problems.

Camping in the garden, riding bikes through the woods, climbing trees, collecting bugs, picking wildflowers, running through piles of autumn leaves...For a whole generation of today's children the pleasures of a free-range childhood are missing, and their indoor habits contribute to epidemic obesity, attention-deficit disorder, isolation and childhood depression.

(back cover)

He goes on to say:

SECTION II

In a survey of the families of ADHD children aged seven to twelve, parents or guardians were asked to identify afterschool or weekend activities that left their children functioning especially well or particularly poorly. Activities were coded as "green" or "not green". Green activities, for example, included camping and fishing. Not-green activities included watching television, playing video games, doing homework...They found that greenery in a child's everyday environment, even views of green through a window, specifically reduces attention deficit symptoms.

(p 106)

As I continued to read, I discovered that many of the suggestions to reduce the symptoms of ADHD had been in place in the behavioural unit in Wayne's previous school.

- A view of nature: the classroom looked out onto a garden specifically created for the children.

- "Green playgrounds": the children spent their breaks not with the rest of the pupils but in the class garden.

- Plant and care for trees and vegetation: the children in the unit planted and nurtured the plants in the garden, which they were developing as a nature conservation area. The area was already attracting a variety of birds and squirrels, which the children loved to watch.

I wondered if this had played a part in Wayne's progress whilst he was there.

SECTION II

Rosefield, his present school, was finding it hard to appoint a teaching assistant to support Wayne; I suspected because the salary on offer and the skills required didn't really add up. Six weeks at home became seven, and so on, until eventually it was Easter. Then came the news that someone had been found to fill the post; they would come and meet Wayne at home and then a gradual reintegration back into school would begin. This came as a huge relief. Even when he wasn't around, I found I was rapidly losing the ability to focus on anything for more than a few minutes at a time. I was becoming forgetful, confused and I jokingly said I was developing ADHD, though part of me thought that it wasn't a joke at all!

At last the day arrived when the Head of Rosefield came to the house to introduce Stephen, who was to be Wayne's full-time teaching assistant. When they arrived I didn't know whether to laugh or cry. Stephen was an 18-year-old with no previous experience of working with children. Even at home, where Wayne was relatively calm, he immediately started to outwit Stephen. I could see that through no fault of his, Stephen had been set up to fail. He was a lovely young man, who clearly wanted to do the right thing, but Wayne needed someone who could maintain firm boundaries, keep one step ahead and also had experience of dealing with young people with Wayne's type of difficulties.

Within a few weeks it became obvious that reintegrating Wayne back into school wasn't going to happen any time soon. An interim review of his Statement of Special Educational Needs identified that in the school's opinion he needed the support of two full-time teaching assistants working in rotation throughout the day. The local education authority didn't agree with the school's assessment and we weren't even sure that this school was able to meet Wayne's educational needs. He needed a small environment which was relatively calm and had a predictable structure and routine. We were given permission to start looking for an alternative.

Rosefield was moving to a new purpose-built site in September and it was agreed that Wayne would remain at home until then, and if we didn't find another suitable alternative he would rejoin at their new premises at the start of the next academic year. The local education authority did suggest a few other schools we could consider, but they all seemed too much like Rosefield, and didn't seem to offer any advantages. It was looking increasingly likely that Wayne would be staying at Rosefield, and whilst we were describing him as being much calmer, we were, of course, meaning Wayne's version of calm, and felt that without the right support things could still go wrong.

September came and with the support of two new teaching support assistants Wayne returned to Rosefield, in its new state of the art building. He had hardly been in school for more than a couple of hours when the telephone rang. 'Mrs Miles, I am really sorry but we have had to exclude Wayne. The removers left a trolley in the corridor and Wayne has used it as a skateboard and has been hurtling around the corridors. We can't allow this for health and safety reasons'. I had to smile at Wayne's ingenuity and questioned the wisdom of leaving such an item in the corridor in the first place, but reluctantly went to collect him.

Over the following weeks there were a number of occasions when Wayne was excluded, or sent home early. He quite rightly got a five-day exclusion for throwing a chair across the classroom in anger; I used the time when he was at home to reinforce the work we had done previously on anger management and this time Wayne seemed to get it. But less than a week later, I got a call to say he had been excluded for five days again. When I arrived at school, Wayne ran up to me and excitedly told me that I would be proud of him. He said that he had thought about the anger management strategies we had worked on and instead of throwing something which would hurt someone he had thrown a cushion. I was really pleased that he had taken the time to think things through and had made a better choice than previously; as far as I was concerned it was progress. But the Head said that the school rule was "No throwing" and the exclusion stood. As soon as Wayne heard this he turned to the Head and responded with 'F*** you, next time I'll throw the chair!' Secretly, I had to agree with him, and let the Head know my view when we next met to review Wayne's progress.

If one or other of the teaching support assistants was absent for any reason, Wayne wasn't allowed in school. Often the phone call advising me of this was minutes before his taxi arrived, and I would have to send it away again. We didn't know from one day to the next whether Wayne would be going to school or not. He found the situation really unsettling and became agitated even before he left home. Once he arrived at school he was ushered into a room where he was expected to 'calm himself down' before joining his class after registration. He didn't join the rest of the school at break time but was allowed to sit by the window in the classroom and watch the other children play so that he could 'watch and learn how to behave'.

The situation was desperate and once again at breaking point. We were well aware that if we couldn't find suitable education, the placement would have to end. Tim and I felt that if this was going to happen, and Wayne was going to have to move to a residential setting, we wanted to know that we had tried everything we could. Medication was once again mentioned, and faced with the choice of Wayne moving on or giving the medication a go, we felt we had no alternative. My mind was in turmoil as I struggled to sort out how much of Wayne's behaviour related to each of the possible causes. Trauma?... Attachment?...ADHD? Was this the right route to go down? My final conclusion was: did it really matter? We were only going to trial the medication; if it didn't work, we wouldn't be continuing, so why not give it a try?

There had been quite a lot of publicity about how some children with ADHD had been helped by omega-3 fish oil in capsule form and I had already been giving Wayne this, but the only obvious improvement was shining hair and strong nails. In a last feeble attempt to back out and avoid stronger drugs, I asked the paediatrician if an increased dose of omega-3 would help. She was sympathetic but said that there was little evidence to suggest that it would make a real difference. So after she had examined, weighed and measured Wayne, we left her consulting room with me clutching a prescription for Concerta, a prolonged (slow) release form of methylphenidate hydrochloride, and feeling physically sick. As I stood in the chemist waiting for the prescription to be made up, I was conscious of everyone around me. Did other people know what drug I was getting? Did they think I was a dreadful parent? What was the pharmacist thinking about me? Could I pretend to give Wayne the drug and then claim it hadn't worked?

That evening when Wayne was in bed, I read the leaflet that came with the Concerta. The paediatrician had told me that one of the problems with the drug was that it could suppress appetite and slow down growth but as I read the leaflet my heart sank even further. One in 10 people could experience palpitations, one in 100, hearing, seeing or feeling things which are not real, or uncontrolled body movements. The list went on and on and I was rapidly going off the idea of even trying it.

It had been agreed that we would start the medication at the weekend when Tim would also be around, and so on Saturday morning, with my hand physically shaking, I gave Wayne the first dose. By lunchtime, alongside anxiety that perhaps I was overlooking a dangerous side effect, I thought that perhaps Wayne did seem calmer. But then he knew about the purpose of the medication and had been really keen to try it, so perhaps it was a placebo effect?

As the days passed we noticed a marked difference in Wayne's behaviour: he was still very active and lively but he did seem to be able to concentrate and focus better, making choices which were a little more considered. But the school reported they had noticed no difference. We suspected that they had had enough of Wayne and were pushing for him to move on. The fact that Wayne wasn't welcome was confirmed when the Head rang me about the official opening of the school. She explained that the children would be putting on a performance for the mayor, other local dignitaries and councillors and that it 'wouldn't be suitable for Wayne to attend'. Like us, Wayne was devastated at this news and this, coupled with the fact that he was now only in school for about an hour a day, made us determined that no matter what the outcome was, and even if it meant a residential setting, we had to find alternative education for him.

The local education authority said that we had exhausted all options and we were in despair when a chance conversation with one of Tim's nieces, whom we hadn't seen for some time, gave us hope. She told us about an independent special needs school, The Castle, which is based on Rudolf Steiner principles and located within a reasonable daily driving distance. As soon as we looked at the school we knew it was right for Wayne. It is set in extensive grounds and much of the curriculum is taught outdoors. Subjects include estate work, gardening, woodwork, bakery skills and other practical activities. Time is spent outside first thing in the morning before the literacy and numeracy sessions begin and cycling and trampolining are on the break-time agenda. With only five children in a class and a teacher who moves up with the children every year to reduce change…it seemed perfect.

It took four months of wrangling, debate and a few strongly worded letters threatening to take legal action before the education authority agreed funding but finally, just before Easter 2008, Wayne joined The Castle school and settled in almost immediately.

As Wayne seemed to be responding to the medication, and his weight and appetite hadn't been affected, it was agreed to keep him on Concerta during this transition period. Wayne himself was also noticing the difference and was now referring to it as his "concentration pill". We certainly noticed a difference in his impulsivity and ability to focus if we forgot to give it to him. The only downside was what is sometimes known as a "kickback" period in the evening, when the effects of the drug are wearing off and intense hyperactivity follows. Initially this had caused Wayne some sleep problems, but a prescription for melatonin soon sorted this out and resulted in Wayne getting the best sleep he had ever had, with the added bonus that the nightmares which had haunted him for several years also stopped.

After a settled two years in education, and with Wayne really starting to form an attachment to us, we decided that over the summer holidays of 2010 we would try gradually to reduce the Concerta with a view to him either being on a reduced dose or possibly off medication completely by the start of the new academic year. But one week into the holidays, whilst on a day out with Wayne, I had a fall which resulted in me spending two weeks in hospital and the rest of the summer in a wheelchair recovering. Wayne was so worried that it didn't seem to be the right time to start adjusting his medication and adding to his anxiety. That plan remains on hold.

So after over 20 years in contact with children with ADHD, what are my thoughts on the subject today? Current thinking suggests that ADHD is largely genetic and due to an imbalance of some of the neurotransmitter chemicals in the brain; there is some debate on whether home life can influence these predetermined factors. This to me seems a much more reasonable explanation than just home life and diet alone, and would account for the fact that a change to more appropriate parenting and food, in my experience, makes no difference at all.

Having seen the real improvement that medication has made in Wayne's life, I have to confess that I feel very guilty that I denied him access to it for so long. Although this was a team decision, perhaps I allowed my own issues with drugs to cloud my thinking, and didn't pursue the matter in the way that I should have done. I am still not sure that medication is the right thing with regard to the longer term outcomes and I worry about the future, but there is no doubt that it has made a real difference to Wayne's life. Having said this, I think it is important to bear in mind the impact that attachment issues and trauma can have on children like Wayne and not to rush to the conclusion that ADHD is the problem.

My advice on parenting a child with ADHD:

- **Look after yourself** This really is a priority: it's not selfish, it's essential. Parenting a child with ADHD can be exhausting, demoralising and frustrating; you cannot give the child what he or she needs if you are short-tempered and tearing your hair out. It is all too easy to use any moments of freedom from caring to catch up with all those domestic tasks that have been piling up, but don't lose sight of the wider world and become isolated. Taking time for yourself to enjoy nature, to appreciate art or music, for meditation, yoga, martial arts, prayer, both shared and individual, and many physical activities can help you build resilience and prevent undue stress. Sometimes finding the motivation to do this can be hard; as our stress levels increase, our motivation decreases, and we get caught in a vicious circle. Engage the help of a partner or friend to encourage you to get out and get going.

SECTION II

- **Focus on the positive things** Each day, take time to think of the positive things, perhaps jot them down in your diary or a notebook, write them on post-it notes and create a "positive" wall. Don't think too big: sometimes the positives can be minute but represent huge progress for the child. Share the positives with the child and help them to think about the positives from each day. All too often, all they hear are negative comments about themselves, which further undermine their feelings of self-worth. Photographs of good times, notes about the things you like and enjoy about your child or things they think they are good at can all be added to the "positive" wall or to a scrap book as a reminder that things are not all bad.

- **Be realistic** Rome wasn't built in a day. You can't expect to change everything at once. Focus on just one or two behaviours at a time – those that are really important to you. If you try to change too many things at once, some are bound to not work out, and both you and the child may end up feeling that you have failed.

- **Be specific** Explain clearly what you want the child to do. 'Don't play in the road' will mean just that and won't help them to know where they can play. 'Play on the pavement or in the garden' is clear and leaves no room for misinterpretation. 'Put all the books on the bookshelf and the toys in the box' is so much better than just saying 'Tidy your room'. Remember that children with ADHD often have appalling memories and get distracted really easily so don't give a long list of instructions in one go.

- **Don't nag** Use lists or pictorial prompts to remind the child about everyday tasks and chores. A picture of someone swimming or cooking stuck on the front door handle can remind them of things they need to take to school for specific activities. Unfortunately, it won't stop them leaving their kit in the taxi or under a bush in the playground!

- **Don't get sucked into arguments** Often children with ADHD can argue for England and just have to have the last word. Be firm, be clear and then walk away. Even if you are just repeatedly saying 'no' or 'I've told you already', the child is controlling you, not the other way around. The child will feed off your anger so the more wound up you get, the more the child's temper will escalate. For things like television, mobile phones and computer games, writing a contract with the rules and sanctions for flouting them, which both you and the child sign, can be helpful and avoids the child saying 'But I didn't know'.

- **Stick to routines** Familiarity and structure both help to create a feeling of safety and reduce the child's anxiety. This can be particularly relevant for children who also have attachment issues and who have missed the structure and routine of the early years. Planning any change to their routine well in advance and explaining the reasons for the change can also help.

- **Talk about it** Explain about their ADHD to the child and to everyone the child comes into contact with. Knowing that they are not "bad" and not to blame for the problems can be a real boost to children's self-esteem. Explain as much as you can about the condition to other children in the family, so that they can understand why the rules may be different for them. Use your support networks to talk about the impact that caring is having on you, be clear about what support you need, and don't expect people to guess at what you need because everyone is different.

- **Set things up to succeed** Hard as it is, you may have to do things differently to how you would like or have always done them. If the child finds it hard to sit at the table waiting for a meal, it's no good taking them to a restaurant where food is cooked to order and service is slow! You may not really agree with children watching DVDs in the car instead of admiring the passing scenery, but it if gets you from A to B without the child stressing out everyone else in the car, it could be worth it.

- **Get outdoors, get active** Even if you live in the city, try and get your child out and into green spaces as often as you can. If it's wet or there is nowhere suitable nearby, put on a CD or the radio, turn it up loud and get dancing! It's a great way for the child to release energy and a good way for you to de-stress too.

- **Don't beat yourself up** We all get bad days when we lose our temper, don't respond as we should or feel so exhausted that we go and buy a take-away instead of cooking a meal – that's part of being human, not an indicator of failure. Treat each day as a new beginning and don't dwell on what went wrong the day before. Comments such as 'I hope you are going to behave better than yesterday' or 'Don't start that again' aren't helpful.

Remember: every day may not be a good one, but there is something good in every day.

References

Feingold BF (1975) *Why Your Child is Hyperactive,* New York, NY: Random House

Levine PA and Kline M (2007) *Trauma through a Child's Eyes: Awakening the ordinary miracle of healing,* California: North Atlantic Books

Louv R (2005) *Last Child in the Woods: Saving our children from Nature-Deficit Disorder,* London: Atlantic Books

SECTION II

References

ADDISS (2003) *Parents, Provision and Policy: A consultation with parents,* available at: http://addiss.co.uk/factsheets.htm

Adey P, Hewitt G, Hewitt J and Landau N (2004) *The Professional Development of Teachers: Practice and theory,* London: Kluwer

APA (1994) *Diagnostic and Statisitical Manual (DSM-IV),* Washington DC: American Psychiatric Association

Blachman DR and Hinshaw SP (2002) 'Patterns of friendship among girls with and without attention-deficit/hyperactivity disorder', *Journal of Abnormal Child Psychology,* 30, pp 625–640

Block J and Smith M (2010) *ADD/ADHD and School,* available at: http://helpguide.org/mental/adhd_add_teaching_strategies.htm

Carter CM, Urbanowicz M, Hemsley R, Mantilla L, Strobel S, Graham PJ and Taylor E (1993) 'Effects of a few food diet in attention deficit disorder', *Archives of Disease in Childhood*, 69(5), pp 564–568

Collishaw S, Maughan B, Goodman R and Pickles A (2004) 'Time trends in adolescent mental health', *Journal of Child Psychology and Psychiatry*, 45, pp 1350–1362

Cooper P and Ideus K (1996) *Attention Deficit/Hyperactivity Disorder: A practical guide for teachers*, London: David Fulton

Curran S (2007) 'Biological foundations', in Taylor E (ed) *People with Hyperactivity: Understanding and managing their problems*, London: Mac Keith Press

Egger J, Carter CM, Graham PJ, Gumley D and Soothill JF (1985) 'Controlled trial of oligoantigenic treatment in the hyperkinetic syndrome', *Lancet*, 1:8428, pp 540–545

Farrington DP (1995) 'The twelfth Jack Tizzard Memorial Lecture. The development of offending and antisocial behaviour from childhood: key findings from the Cambridge Study in Delinquent Development', *Journal of Child Psychology and Psychiatry*, 36, pp 929–964

Feingold BF (1975) *Why Your Child is Hyperactive*, New York, NY: Random House

Hoza B (2007) 'Peer functioning in children with ADHD', *Journal of Pediatric Psychology Special Issue on Attention-Deficit/Hyperactivity Disorder*, 32:6, pp 655–663

Hoza B, Mrug S, Gerdes AC, Hinshaw SP, Bukowski WM, Gold JA and Arnold LE (2005) 'What aspects of peer relationships are impaired in children with Attention-Deficit/Hyperactivity Disorder?', *Journal of Consulting & Clinical Psychology*, 73:3, pp 411–423

Jensen PS, Kettle L, Roper MT, Sloan MT, Dulcan MK, Hoven C and Payne JD (1999) 'Are stimulants overprescribed? Treatment of ADHD in four US communities', *Journal of the American Academy of Child & Adolescent Psychiatry*, 38:7, pp 797–804

Klein RG and Mannuzza S (1991) 'Long-term outcome of hyperactive children: a review', *Journal of the American Academy of Child & Adolescent Psychiatry*, 30:3, pp 383–387

Lahey BB, Pelham WE, Loney J, Kipp H, Ehrhardt A, Lee SS and Massetti G (2004) 'Three-year predictive validity of DSM-IV attention deficit hyperactivity disorder in children diagnosed at 4–6 years of age', *American Journal of Psychiatry*, 161:11, pp 2014–2020

Levine PA and Kline M (2007) *Trauma through a Child's Eyes: Awakening the ordinary miracle of healing*, California: North Atlantic Books

Louv R (2005) *Last Child in the Woods: Saving our children from Nature-Deficit Disorder,* London: Atlantic Books

McCann D, Barrett A, Cooper A, Crumpler D, Dalen L, Grimshaw K and Stevenson J (2007) 'Food additives and hyperactive behaviour in 3-year-old and 8/9-year-old children in the community: a randomised, double-blinded, placebo-controlled trial', *Lancet*, 370:9598, pp 1560–1567

Mikami AY, Jack A, Emeh CC and Stephens HF (2010) 'Parental influence on children with attention-deficit/hyperactivity disorder: I. Relationships between parent behaviors and child peer status', *Journal of Abnormal Child Psychology*, 38:6, pp 721–736

Munden A and Arcelus J (1999) *The AD/HD Handbook: A handbook for parents and professionals on attention deficit/hyperactivity disorder*, London: Jessica Kingsley Publishers

NICE (2008) CG72 *Attention Deficit hyperactivity Disorder: full guidance*, available at: http://guidance.nice.org.uk/CG72/Guidance/pdf/English

NICE and SCIE (2006) 'Parent-training/education programmes in the management of children with conduct disorders', *Technology Appraisal*, 102, available at: www.nice.org.uk/TA102

O'Connor TG, Heron J, Golding J, Beveridge M and Glover V (2002) 'Maternal antenatal anxiety and children's behavioural/emotional problems at 4 years: report from the Avon Longitudinal Study of Parents and Children', *British Journal of Psychiatry*, 180, pp 502–508

Parker HC (1999) *Put Yourself in their Shoes: Understanding teenagers with Attention Deficit Hyperactivity Disorder*, Plantation, FL: Specialty Press Inc

Patterson GR and Forgatch MS (2005a) *Parents And Adolescents Living Together: Part 1, The basics* (2nd ed. Vol. 1), Champaign, IL: Research Press

Patterson GR and Forgatch MS (2005b) *Parents And Adolescents Living Together: Part 2, Family problem solving* (2nd ed. Vol. 2), Champaign, IL: Research Press

Poulton A (2006) 'Growth and sexual maturation in children and adolescents with attention deficit hyperactivity disorder', *Current Opinion in Pediatrics*, 18, pp 427–434

Rutter M, Roy P and Kreppner J (2002) 'Institutional care as a risk factor for inattention/overactivity', in Sandberg S (ed) *Hyperactivity and Attention Disorders of Childhood* (2nd ed), Cambridge: Cambridge University Press, pp 417–434

Safer DJ (2000) 'Are stimulants overprescribed for youths with ADHD?', *Annals of Clinical Psychiatry*, 12:1, pp 55–62, doi: 10.1023/a:1009031211900

Sayal K (2007) 'Diagnosis and assessment', In Taylor E (ed), *People with Hyperactivity: Understanding and managing their problems*, London: Mac Keith Press

Sayal K, Taylor E, Beecham J and Byrne P (2002) 'Pathways to care in chiuldren at risk of attention-deficit hyperactivity disorder', *British Journal of Psychiatry*, 181, pp 43–48

Schachar RJ, Tannock R, Cunningham C and Corkum PV (1997) 'Behavioral, situational, and temporal effects of treatment of ADHD with methylphenidate', *Journal of the American Academy of Child & Adolescent Psychiatry*, 36:6, pp 754–763

Sibley MH, Pelham WE, Molina BSG, Gnagy EM, Waschbusch DA, Biswas A, MacLean MG, Babinski DE and Karch KM (2011) 'The delinquency outcomes of boys with ADHD with and without comorbidity', *Journal of Abnormal Child Psychology*, 39:1, pp 21–32

Sinclair M (2007) 'Education and advice', in Taylor E (ed) *People with Hyperactivity: Understanding and managing their problems*, London: Mac Keith Press

Sinn N and Bryan J (2007) 'Effect of supplementation with polyunsaturated fatty acids and micronutrients on learning and behavior problems assiciated with child ADHD', *Journal of Developmental and Behavioral Pediatrics*, 28, pp 82–91

Steer C (2010) 'Strategies for primary school teachers, 2011', available at: www.netdoctor.co.uk/adhd/strategiesforprimaryschoolteachers.htm

Taylor E (2007) 'Clinical and epidemiological foundations', in Taylor E (ed) *People with Hyperactivity: Understanding and managing their problems*, London: Mac Keith Press, pp 262

Taylor E and Sonuga-Barke E (2008) 'Disorders of attention and activity', in Rutter M, Bishop D, Pine D, Scott S, Stevenson J, Taylor E, Thapar A (eds) *Child and Adolescent Psychiatry* (5th ed), London: Wiley-Blackwell, pp 521–542

WHO (1992) *International Statistical Classification of Diseases and Related Health Problems* (10th ed (ICD-10)), Geneva: World Health Organisation

Wilens TE, Faraone SV, Biederman J and Gunawardene S (2003) 'Does stimulant therapy of attention-deficit/hyperactivity disorder beget later substance abuse? A meta-analytic review of the literature', *Pediatrics*, 111:1, pp 179–185

Useful organisations

There are several sources of help for a child with ADHD/ hyperkinetic disorder.

- As an adopter or carer, you may have access to fostering support or to post-adoption support. Contact your social worker for more information.

- Your general practitioner should be able to refer you to a Child and Adolescent Mental Health Service (CAMHS) to see a child and adolescent psychiatrist or specialist nurse, or to a paediatrician with an interest in ADHD.

- You may be eligible for Government allowances – ask your social worker, your local authority social services department, your nearest Citizens Advice Bureau or call the Benefits Enquiry Helpline on 0800 882200.

- For education advice, consult your local authority, or alternatively the Advisory Centre for Education (ACE) (www.ace-ed.org.uk/, helpline: 0808 800 5793) or Independent Parental Special Needs Advice (IPSA) (www.ipsea.org.uk/, helpline: 0800 018 4016)

National Attention Deficit Disorder Information and Support Service (ADDISS)

Provides user-friendly information and resources about ADHD to anyone who needs assistance, including parents, carers, sufferers, teachers or health professionals.

Premier House
112 Station Road
Edgware
Middlesex HA8 7BJ
Tel: 020 8952 2800
www.addiss.co.uk

ADDERS

Promotes awareness of ADHD and provides information, advice and links to support groups for both adults and children and their families.
www.adders.org

Contact a Family

Provides support, advice and information for families with disabled children, no matter what their condition or disability.

209–211 City Road
London EC1V 1JN
Tel: 020 7608 8700
Helpline: 0808 808 3555
www.cafamily.org.uk